Things I Like

I Like Dinosaurs

Angela Aylmore

Heinemann Library
Chicago, Illinois

Customer Service 888–454–2279
Visit our website at www.heinemannlibrary.com

Photo research by Erica Newbery
Designed by Joanna Hinton-Malivoire
Printed in China by South China Printing Company Limited

11 10 09 08 07
10 9 8 7 6 5 4 3 2 1

Library of Congress Cataloging-in-Publication Data
Aylmore, Angela.
  I like dinosaurs / Angela Aylmore.
     p. cm. -- (Things I like)
  Includes bibliographical references and index.
  ISBN-13: 978-1-4034-9264-7 (lib. bdg.)
  ISBN-10: 1-4034-9264-6 (lib. bdg.)
  ISBN-13: 978-1-4034-9273-9 (pbk.)
  ISBN-10: 1-4034-9273-5 (pbk.)
  1. Dinosaurs--Juvenile literature. I. Title.
  QE861.5.A95 2007
  567.9--dc22

                                          2006024843

Acknowledgments
The publishers would like to thank the following for permission to reproduce photographs: Alamy pp. **9** (David R. Frazier Photolibrary, Inc.), **20** (Steven May), **21** (Brand X Pictures), **22** (Steven May); NHPA pp. **18–19**.

Illustrations by James Field of Simon Girling and Associates.

Cover photograph of a Tyrannosaurus rex skeleton reproduced with permission of Corbis (Louie Psihoyos).

Every effort has been made to contact copyright holders of any material reproduced in this book. Any omissions will be rectified in subsequent printings if notice is given to the publisher.

Contents

Some words are shown in bold, **like this**. You can find out what they mean by looking in the Glossary.

Dinosaurs

I like dinosaurs. Dinosaurs are animals that lived a very long time ago.

Tyrannosaurus Rex

My favorite dinosaur is
Tyrannosaurus rex.

It had very sharp teeth.
These helped it to attack
other dinosaurs.

Tyrannosaurus rex had very small arms. Each arm had two fingers.

I like to look at Tyrannosaurus rex bones at the **museum**.

Velociraptor

Velociraptor was a small dinosaur. It was even smaller than you.

Scientists think it could run
as fast as a car.

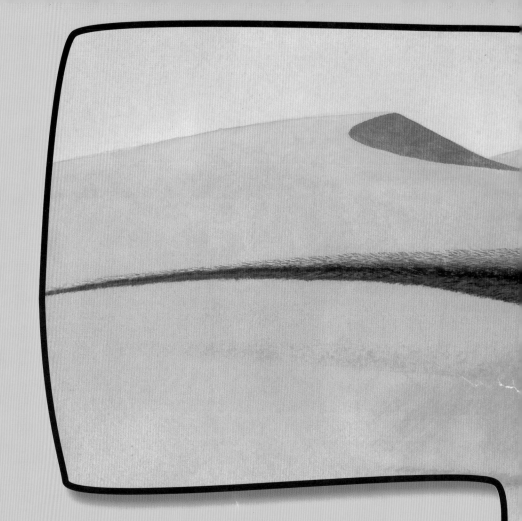

Even though Velociraptor was small, it was still dangerous. It had very sharp teeth and claws.

Triceratops

This dinosaur is Triceratops.
I think it looks like a rhino.

Triceratops means "horrible three-horned face."

Triceratops ate plants.

Triceratops laid eggs. The eggs **hatched** into baby Triceratops.

Dinosaur Fossils

This is a dinosaur **fossil.**
Fossils tell us what the
dinosaurs looked like.

You can see dinosaur fossils in some **museums**.

Have you ever found a fossil?

Do You Like Dinosaurs?

Now you know why I like dinosaurs! Do you like dinosaurs, too?

Glossary

fossil remains of a plant or animal, usually found in rocks

hatch to come out of an egg

museum building where people can see artistic, historic, or scientific objects

Find Out More

Mattern, Joanne. *Dinosaur Tails and Armor.* Milwaukee: Gareth Stevens, 2006.

Matthews, Rupert. *Tyrannosaurus Rex.* Chicago: Heinemann Library, 2003.

Index